THE GOLDILOCKS ZONE

CONDITIONS NECESSARY FOR EXTRATERRESTRIAL LIFE

LAURA LA BELLA

ROSEN
PUBLISHING

NEW YORK

Published in 2016 by The Rosen Publishing Group, Inc.
29 East 21st Street, New York, NY 10010

Copyright © 2016 by The Rosen Publishing Group, Inc.

First Edition

Library of Congress Cataloging-in-Publication Data

Names: La Bella, Laura, author.
Title: The Goldilocks zone : conditions necessary for extraterrestrial life /
  Laura La Bella.
Description: First edition. | New York : Rosen Publishing, 2016. |
  Series: The search for other Earths | Audience: Grades 7-12. | Includes
  bibliographical references and index.
Identifiers: LCCN 2015033905 | ISBN 9781499462982 (library bound)
Subjects: LCSH: Habitable planets--Juvenile literature. | Extrasolar
  planets--Juvenile literature. | Life on other planets--Juvenile literature.
Classification: LCC QB820 .L3 2016 | DDC 523.2/4--dc23
LC record available at http://lccn.loc.gov/2015033905

Manufactured in China

CONTENTS

INTRODUCTION

Earth sits more than 92 million miles from the sun, in a Goldilocks zone, or region where the conditions are just right to support life on our planet.

re we alone?

Is there life beyond Earth?

Will we be able to live on other planets someday?

These are questions astrophysicists, astronomers, researchers, astrobiologists, and other scientists have been asking for decades about planets not only in our solar system but those found across our vast universe.

The discovery of more than a thousand confirmed planets that orbit around stars similar to our sun has intrigued researchers, scientists, and the public for years. The intense interest for the public may be more about the idea that another intelligent life-form exists beyond our human race. But for scientists who are searching for planets with similar atmospheres as Earth, which might be able to support life, the question is not if life exists elsewhere but rather when we might discover it.

And by "life," scientists don't necessarily mean human life, another humanlike species, or even intelligent alien life. Astrophysicists and astronomers are looking for extrasolar planets with atmospheres that can support even the smallest forms of life, such as microorganisms, bacteria, and microbes. They are also looking for planets where liquid water and other natural resources may be found.

Scientists first believed that the conditions for human life to survive on another planet needed to be near perfect to what we have here on Earth. Those criteria—an atmosphere that is oxygen-rich, moderate surface and atmospheric temperatures consistent with our own, and the existence of liquid water—have led researchers to look for planets in what they call the Goldilocks zone, or an area of space where a planet is located just the right distance from its home star so that the planet's surface is not too hot and not too cold.

Since the discovery of numerous planets and the study of their planetary surfaces, as well as research here on Earth, researchers have come to redefine the types and kinds of environments that can support life. While the ideal is still to find a planet in the Goldilocks zone of not too hot and not too cold, scientists have come to discover that even in extreme environments, found right here on Earth, life finds a way to survive and even thrive. Microbes can survive in nuclear reactors, can thrive in skin-searing acid, and can live in boiling-hot water. There are even complete ecosystems that have never seen the light of day and can be so hot that the heat can melt metal. These microbes and environments have changed what scientists thought about life being able to survive elsewhere in the universe.

The discovery of the first exoplanet orbiting a star similar to our sun was made in 1992, and in 1995, scientists were able to confirm that the planet existed in a Goldilocks zone. The discovery and confirmation were both milestones. There have since been significant discoveries and confirmation of exoplanets throughout our solar system and the universe, and more candidate planets have been identified and are awaiting evaluation to see if they, too, reside within a Goldilocks zone. These discoveries and the possibilities that come with them—of life, however small and/or intelligent, of liquid water, and of an atmosphere that can sustain human life—have interested scientists, astronomers, astrophysicists, and the general public.

CHAPTER ONE

IS THERE A NEAR-PERFECT PLANET?

At the moment, life on Earth is the only known life in the Universe, but there are compelling arguments to suggest we are not alone. Indeed, most astrophysicists accept a high probability of there being life elsewhere." This announcement was made by Neil deGrasse Tyson, a leading astrophysicist who is also the director of the Hayden Planetarium at the American Museum of Natural History.

Astrophysicists have been searching for life on other planets by identifying planets that exists in what researchers have defined as the Goldilocks zone.

WHAT IS THE GOLDILOCKS ZONE?

The Goldilocks zone is the region around a star where a planetary-like object with sufficient atmospheric pressure can support liquid water on its surface. The name is also used for planets that are close to the size of Earth, which has a circumference of 24,902 miles (40,000 kilometers), a radius of 3,959 miles (6,370 km), and a diameter is 7,900 miles (12,700 km). Also called the "habitable zone" or the "circumstellar habitable zone," scientists believe the Goldilocks zone is where we might find life to exist beyond our own planet. The idea isn't necessary to find a perfect match to Earth but to identify a planet that has the right conditions in its biosphere to support various forms of life.

WHY IS IT CALLED THE GOLDILOCKS ZONE?

More than four billion years ago, our solar system formed around a giant star—the sun—that was radiating heat. Some planets formed too close to the sun, such as Mercury and Venus, making their atmospheres too hot and vaporizing any existence of water on their surfaces. Other planets formed too far away, like Mars, which made its atmosphere too cold and too dry. But Earth formed in just the right spot, where the temperatures were ideal to sustain liquid water and where the atmosphere was comprised of the right balance of oxygen and carbon dioxide. This region around the sun, where Earth exists, is called the Goldilocks zone.

In the fairy tale *Goldilocks and the Three Bears*, Goldilocks is looking for certain things to be just right: a bed to sleep in that is not too hard or too soft, a bowl of porridge that is not too hot or too cold. For scientists, the Goldilocks zone represents the same kind of near-perfect criteria, only they are searching for conditions needed to support life. Scientists believe they need to find conditions that are very similar to those here on Earth: temperatures that are not too hot or too cold for human life to exist or for water to remain in liquid form, and oxygen levels similar to our atmosphere where life, whether it

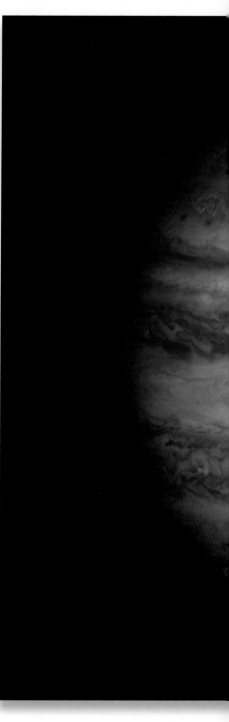

is similar to human life or microscopic, can survive.

PLANETS AND THE UNIVERSE

The universe is made up of planets, stars, matter, and dark matter. There are only two types of planets in the universe: gas giants and terrestrial planets.

Gas giants are planets that consist of giant balls of various gases, such as hydrogen or helium. They have little or no solid surface. The Milky Way, the solar system in which Earth resides, is made up of eight planets, four of which—Jupiter, Saturn, Uranus, and Neptune—are gas giants.

Jupiter, the fifth planet from the sun and the largest planet in our solar system, is a gas giant. It's composed of hydrogen and helium and has a very small rocky core that is uninhabitable.

Gas giants are also ten times the mass of Earth. Mass is the property of a planet that determines the strength of its gravitational pull on other planets. Gas giants are very hot and uninhabitable. They also have very long orbits around their home star, or sun. Jupiter, for example, takes almost twelve Earth years to orbit the sun.

Terrestrial planets are planets that possess heavy-metal cores surrounded by a rocky mantle. Terrestrial planets tend to stick close to their host stars, which means they have smaller orbits and much shorter years. The terrestrial planets in our solar system are Mercury, Venus, Earth, and Mars.

Mars, for example, may be located within the Goldilocks zone, but it is not habitable to human life. The planet's temperature ranges from 70 degrees Fahrenheit (21 degrees Celsius) during Mars's "summer" months to -195°F (-126°C). There is also evidence that water once flowed underground. There is also little oxygen on Mars, which means humans cannot breathe the air on Mars. While Mars

This image of a small trench dug by the Phoenix Mars Lander's Surface Stereo Imager shows a trench, nicknamed "Dodo-Goldilocks," with a white substance scientists think could be ice.

may not support human life, there is evidence that other life-forms may exist on the planet. Studying Mars's atmosphere provides some hope that conditions for life exist on others planets someplace in the universe as well.

Venus, the second-closest planet to the sun after Mercury, is often called Earth's sister planet because both are about the same size, have nearly identical masses, and are made of almost the same materials. Venus also sits in the sun's Goldilocks zone. But the atmosphere of Venus is far different from that of Earth. The planet is completely covered by thick clouds, which traps carbon dioxide and creates an intensive greenhouse effect. The

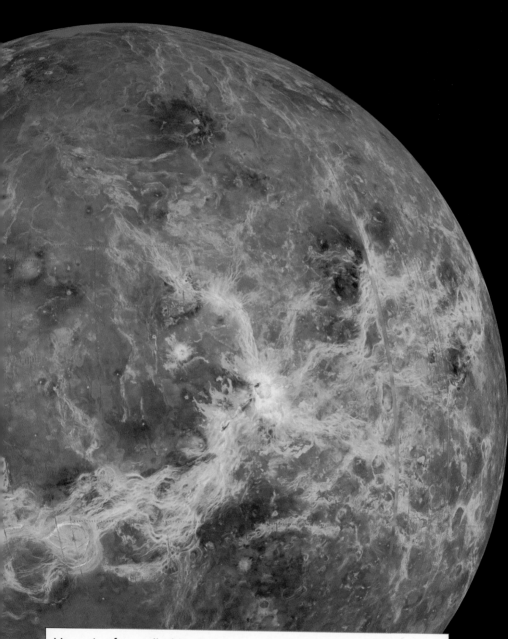

Venus is often called Earth's "sister planet" because they are both of similar size, mass, composition, and proximity to the sun.

Environmental Protection Agency explains the greenhouse effect in this way: "The Earth gets energy from the sun in the form of sunlight. The Earth's surface absorbs some of this energy and heats up. That's why the surface of a road can

OUR GALAXY: THE MILKY WAY

The Milky Way is the galaxy that contains our solar system. A solar system is comprised of a sun and the objects that orbit it. In the Milky Way, our sun is orbited by eight planets: Mercury, Venus, Earth, Mars, Jupiter, Saturn, Uranus, and Neptune. The Milky Way:

- Contains more than 200 billion stars.
- Was made from the collision of several other galaxies.
- Has a black hole at its center.
- Is 13.6 billion years old, which is almost as old as the universe itself.
- Is warped. The galaxy is elliptical, like a disc, not circular.
- Is mostly made up of dust, gasses, and dark matter.
- Is always moving in space.
- Is one of billions of galaxies in the universe.

feel hot even after the sun has gone down—because it has absorbed a lot of energy from the sun. The Earth cools down by giving off a different form of energy, called infrared radiation. But before all this radiation can escape to outer space, greenhouse gases in the atmosphere absorb some of it, which makes the atmosphere warmer. As the atmosphere gets warmer, it makes the Earth's surface warmer, too." On Venus, however, its massive cloud cover makes it impossible for heat to escape its atmosphere, so it radiates back onto the surface of the planet. At 750 degrees Kelvin, or 900°F (480°C), Venus is the hottest planet in our solar system because of its greenhouse effect.

THE EARTH'S BIOSPHERE

As researchers look for signs of life on other planets, they often seek atmospheres with conditions similar to those of Earth's biosphere, the layer of our planet where life exists. Earth has five layers, each with distinct characteristics.

The lithosphere is Earth's outermost shell.

It includes Earth's crust and the uppermost mantle, which is the hard and rigid outer layer of Earth. The hydrosphere is Earth's liquid water, which includes all of our oceans, lakes, rivers, and groundwater. The atmosphere contains air and tiny particles around Earth. The cryosphere refers to all of Earth's frozen places, such as the icy poles, mountain glaciers, frozen soil, sea ice, and seasonal snow.

Earth's biosphere includes all life in the oceans and on all land, including plants, animals, insects, microbes, and humans. It's the layer of Earth where life exists.

All of these spheres work together. NASA's Earth Science Week blog explains that if change happens in one sphere, it affects the other spheres as well. "If winds in the atmosphere shift, weather patterns change. Rain that might normally fall in one place falls in another. The first place dries up. Streams shrink. Plants die, leaving bare soil that is prone to erosion. The

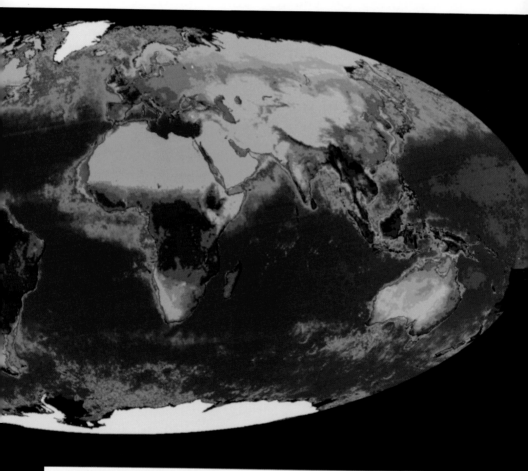

This illustration shows Earth's global biosphere. The image shows areas of vegetation on land and where plantlike organisms live in our oceans.

soil heats up and dries out. As a result, drought will develop."

The sun plays a major role in sustaining life on our planet. Life on Earth depends on the sun. Sunlight provides energy that is captured by plants, some kinds of bacteria, and protists formed in photosynthesis. In photosynthesis, captured energy transforms carbon dioxide into organic compounds such as sugars and produces oxygen. The vast majority of life on Earth, from human life to the incredible array of animal species, fungi, parasitic plants, microbes, and many bacteria, all depend on photosynthesis to survive. It's this model that researchers are looking for when they are searching for planets in the Goldilocks zone that might be able to support human life.

HOW DO PLANETS FORM?

With the formation of the sun, the remaining gas and dust flattened into a rotating protoplanetary disk. Within this swirling debris, rocky particles began to collide, forming larger masses that attracted even more particles via gravity. Gravity caused these particles to contract further to create planetesimals, which collided with one another to become the solid inner planets. Meanwhile, gases froze into giant balls that would build the outer gas giants (planets like Jupiter).

The theory of solar wind tries to explain why rocky planets formed closer to the sun and the gas giants formed farther away. Solar wind is the steady flow of plasma that comes from a star. When the sun first came into being, this wind was far stronger than it is today, strong enough to blast lighter elements such as hydrogen and helium away from the inner orbits. When these elements reached the outer orbits, the strength of the solar wind dropped off. The gravity of the outer gas giants quickly drew those elements in, expanding the gas giants into their current forms: solid cores of rock and ice covered with gas.

But, like all theories, it could be disproved as we study other solar systems. This theory of planetary formation presumes that gas giants always occur in a solar system's outer orbits. In 1995, astronomers discovered the distant planet 51 Pegasi b, a "hot Jupiter," or gas giant, which orbited very close to its sun. This discovery called for new theories, primarily that such planets must form far away from the central star and then move into a closer orbit. Astronomers theorize that such an orbital migration, powered by a gravitational tug of war with other cosmic bodies, would take hundreds of millions of years. The journey would also destroy any smaller, inner planets in its path.

CLUES IN OUR SOLAR SYSTEM

Astronomers say that some 4.5 billion years ago, the universe was nothing but cosmic dust. Our sun was but a fledgling protostar, continually gaining more matter via gravity and steadily cranking up its internal nuclear fusion. There was no solar system, only a giant, rotating cloud of particles called the solar nebula. To figure out how all that leftover gas and dust led to planets, astronomers have studied the structure of our own solar system for clues. They've also looked to distant, younger solar systems still in varying stages of development.

CHAPTER TWO

DEVELOPING THE GOLDILOCKS CONCEPT

Before the Kepler Space Telescope was launched on March 7, 2009, the number of identified exoplanets numbered in the tens and hundreds. At the time, locating a viable exoplanet was extraordinarily difficult. There were significant limitations on the current ground-based telescopes being used, which required that researchers compensate for image distortions that were caused by looking through a lens that had to penetrate Earth's atmosphere. There were plans to create major telescopes aboard space stations and satellites but these were still in development or in the early stages of construction. Much of the search, then, was speculation.

THE GOLDILOCKS CONCEPT

The idea of searching for life on a distant planet has everything to do with the belief that there may be alien life-forms—sentient beings that exist on other planets. As early as the sixth century BCE, a group of people called Pythagoreans, who were followers of a Greek mathematician and philosopher named Pythagoras, believed that the moon was home to living plants and animals. In the fifteenth century, a German astronomer named Nicholas of Cusa suggested that both stars and other parts of "heaven" were also inhabited. Italian Giordano Bruno was burned at the stake for a similar suggestion in 1600. Even William Herschel, an astronomer and the man who discovered Uranus, was said to have believed that the moon, Mars, and the sun were home to thinking creatures.

It didn't end there. Another Italian, Giovanni Schiaparelli, seemed to come up with proof of life on Mars. He looked through a telescope and discovered that the surface of the planet was covered with crisscrossing tracks. This seemed to be confirmed by Percival Lowell, who built a private observatory in Arizona. However, both men were found to be wrong. The images they saw were the result of using telescopes that were too weak. What they saw wasn't really there. That was confirmed by later, stronger telescopes. However, the idea of finding life on another planet still excited some scientists, and in 1959, Philip Morrison of Cornell University and Giuseppe Cocconi proposed that it would be "foolish not to search for the inevitable signals of [extra-terrestrial] civilisations." They did not know how successful a search for extra-terrestrial life would be, but they knew that "if we never search, the chance of success is zero." So the search continued.

Hubertus Strughold, a German-born physiologist and prominent medical researcher, first presented the Goldilocks concept, also known as the circumstellar habitable zone, in 1953, in a paper he wrote called "The Green and the Red Planet: A Physiological Study of the Possibility of Life on Mars." In his paper, Strughold defined various zones in which life could occur. In the same year, Harlow Shapley, an American astronomer who discovered the overall shape of our galaxy, wrote a paper titled "Liquid Water Belt." The paper also suggested that life could exist only in certain areas or zones. Both Strughold and Shapley's theories stressed the importance of the presence of water as a major criteria for supporting life.

But it was Su-Shu Huang, an American astrophysicist, who first used the term "habitable zone," in 1959 to refer to the area around a star where

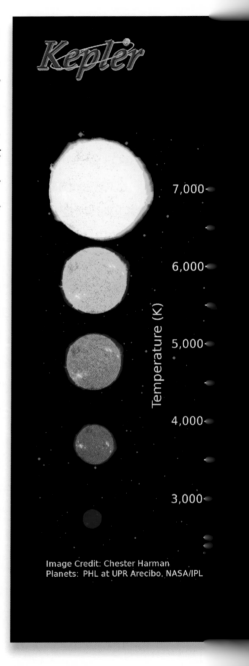

Image Credit: Chester Harman
Planets: PHL at UPR Arecibo, NASA/IPL

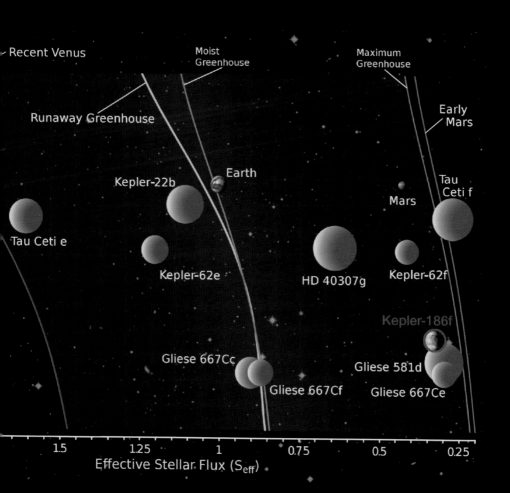

The Habitable Zone

NASA

Recent Venus

Moist Greenhouse

Maximum Greenhouse

Runaway Greenhouse

Early Mars

Kepler-22b

Earth

Tau Ceti f

Mars

Tau Ceti e

Kepler-62e

HD 40307g

Kepler-62f

Kepler-186f

Gliese 667Cc

Gliese 581d

Gliese 667Cf

Gliese 667Ce

1.5   1.25   1   0.75   0.5   0.25

Effective Stellar Flux (S_{eff})

This chart shows planets' relative position to their suns and to the size of other planets in the habitable zone.

liquid water could exist and where life was most likely able to survive. In 1964, the circumstellar habitable zone theory was further enhanced by Stephen H. Dole, who wrote *Habitable Planets for Man*, a book in which he not only wrote about the circumstellar habitable zone, but he also outlined other factors that could support life on other planets. He also estimated the number of habitable planets in the Milky Way to be about 600 million.

It wasn't until the 1970s that the term "Goldilocks zone" emerged as a reference to the specific area around a star whose temperature was "just right" for supporting liquid water on a nearby planet.

In 2000, the theory was updated in *Rare Earth: Why Complex Life Is Uncommon in the Universe*, written by Peter Ward, an American paleontologist, and Donald Brownlee, an astronomer and astrobiologist. In *Rare Earth*, Ward and Brownlee suggest that a galactic habitable zone exists where life is most likely to be found in a galaxy.

THE SETI INSTITUTE

The SETI (Search for Extraterrestrial Intelligence) Institute is a not-for-profit organization whose main purpose, according to the organization's website, is to "explore, understand and explain the origin, nature and prevalence of life in the universe." Located in Mountain View, California, also known as Silicon Valley, one of the most technologically sophisticated regions of the country, the institute employs ground-breaking technological advancements to search for, discover, understand, and explain the nature of life in the universe. SETI focuses its work on three key areas:

Research: SETI is looking for evidence of life in the universe by developing new signal processing algorithms, new search technology, and new search strategies.

Astrobiology: In an attempt to understand more about how life began, SETI is researching diverse forms of life, how they have survived and how they have evolved.

Education and public outreach: Informing the public of their research and discoveries through school-based curriculum for teachers, student internships at the SETI Institute, weekly talks and chats about the latest in search techniques and discoveries, a radio program, and more.

Exploring the billions of planets in the Milky Way is leading scientists to learn more about the formation of our galaxy as well as how Earth and other planets were formed.

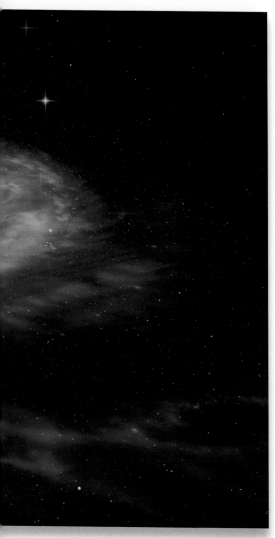

Scientists now know that the concept of life existing only within a Goldilocks zone has been proven false. As researchers used the concept—which relies on the Goldilocks criteria of an oxygen-rich atmosphere, moderate surface temperatures consistent with those of Earth, the existence of liquid water, and a rocky planetary surface—to search for life, they came to find that life existed in several environments that were once considered highly uninhabitable. Scientists have found life, such as bacteria and microbes, in some of the un-likeliest of places: in hot springs, in acid, in sub-freezing tempera-tures, as well as in tem-peratures hot enough to melt metal. These environments have not only shown life can exist there, but in some cases they have thrived.

DISCOVERY OF FIRST EXOPLANET LAUNCHES INTEREST

In 1995, 51 Pegasi b, a gas giant similar to Jupiter that was found to orbit close

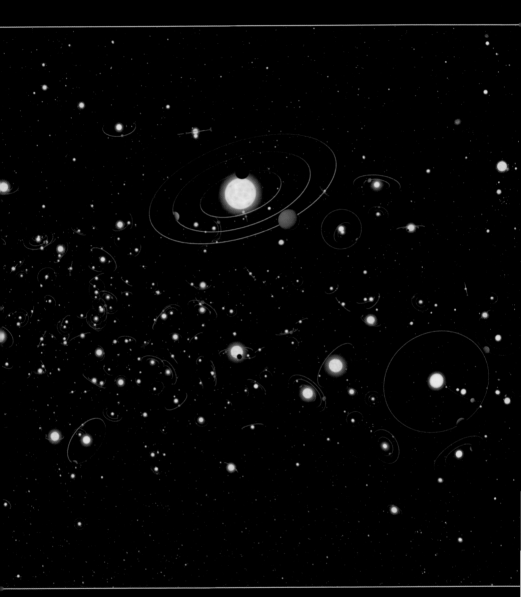

Artistic Impression of Extrasolar Planetary Systems

Research into the position and existence of the billions of other planets in our galaxy may mean that there could be more than one thousand planets within fifty light-years of Earth.

to its parent star, became the first planet ever discovered to orbit a sun-like star. It was a major discovery and launched significant interest in the search for alien, or unknown, planets. It also fueled a change in attitude

NAMING NEW PLANETS

Naming astronomical bodies is the responsibility of the International Astronomical Union (IAU). The IAU, which was founded in 1919, is based in Paris, France. It created a naming system for planets and exoplanets, as well as all celestial bodies, including stars, constellations, supernovae, and galaxies.

The brightest planets of our solar system—Mercury, Venus, Mars, Jupiter, Saturn, Uranus, and Neptune—were named after Roman gods. Later, as other planets were discovered, the IAU put in place a loose naming system in which a proper noun or abbreviation that often corresponds to the name of the host star the planet orbits is used, followed by a lowercase letter (starting with "b"). For example, 51 Pegasi b, the first planet to have ever been discovered orbiting a sun-like star, is named for its constellation, Pegasus, and its position to its sun-like star, b, as its sits in the first position.

among astronomers who had been searching for planets outside our solar system for years.

Debra Fischer, a professor of astronomy at Yale University who has been researching the detection and characterization of exoplanets told *National Geographic* that the discovery of 51 Pegasi b was monumental for her and other scientists like her. "Just before that time,

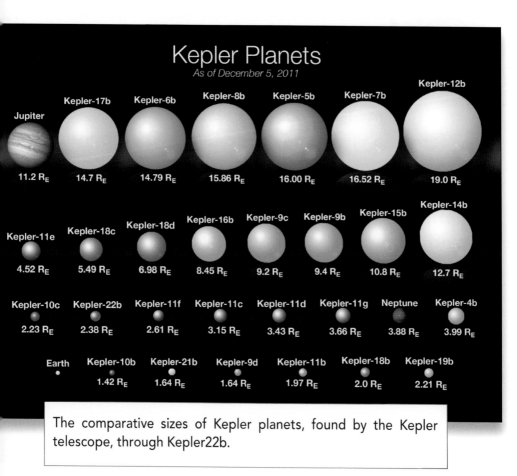

The comparative sizes of Kepler planets, found by the Kepler telescope, through Kepler22b.

I remember astronomers feeling very worried. Scientists had been looking for a long time for exoplanets—for decades—and hadn't found any," she said. "And we really had to step back and say, 'We have to entertain the possibility that maybe the Star Trek picture of the universe isn't right. Maybe there are no other planets around other stars, or they're there rarely.' We now know the universe is teeming with planets. The next step is to figure out if the universe is teeming with life."

The Kepler telescope has since discovered more than 1,800 exoplanets and, based on information from the space telescope reported by astronomers in November 2013, there could be as many as 40 billion Earth-sized planets orbiting in the habitable zones of sun-like stars and red dwarfs just in the Milky Way, the solar system where Earth resides. This doesn't yet account for the massive number of planets that are likely to exist outside of our solar system, in the greater universe itself.

CHAPTER THREE

PLANET HUNTING

The search for planets in the Goldilocks zone has produced a wide range of results with new discoveries occurring more frequently as search techniques improve. In 2014, a planet, called Kepler-186f, was the first Earth-size sphere discovered outside our solar system with an orbit around its sun that is in the Goldilocks zone. Researchers believe the planet to be close in size to Earth, which means it has a strong possibility of having a rocky surface, and that it receives the right amount of radiation from its sun, which means it may have the right temperature to support liquid water.

With advanced planet-hunting techniques and powerful equipment, such as the Kepler

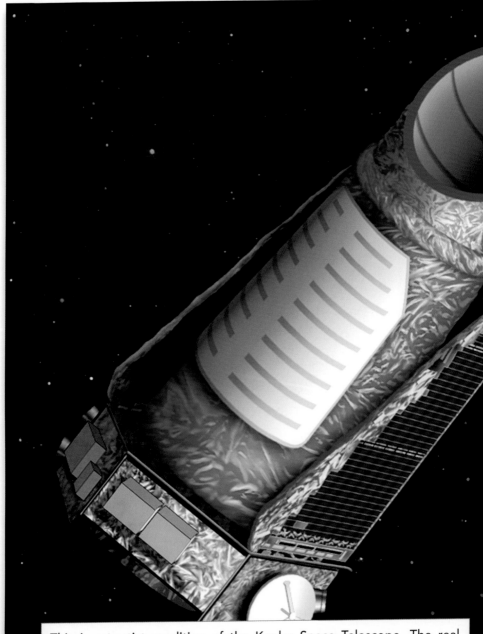

This is an artist rendition of the Kepler Space Telescope. The real Kepler weighs more than 2,300 pounds (1,000 kilograms), can travel 3.6 miles per second (5.8 kilometers per second), and cost more than $550 million to build.

space telescope, astronomers are now able to identify thousands of planets outside of our solar system, which are called exoplanets, and could be within a Goldilocks zone that supports different forms of life. But planet hunting is difficult work and the universe is extremely large.

PLANET DETECTION IS DIFFICULT

Planet hunting is not easy work. Most planets are too small, and many are an immense distance from Earth. They also appear very faint and are overwhelmed by the glare of their parent stars. Even with the largest and most powerful telescopes, it's nearly impossible to detect a planet independently from its sun. However, using massive telescopes with photometers, which measure light, spectrographs, which separate and measure the wavelengths, and infrared

WHY IS PLUTO NO LONGER CONSIDERED A PLANET?

Discovered in 1930, Pluto was known as the smallest planet in the solar system and the ninth planet from the sun, making it an icy, frigid planet. In 2003, an astronomer identified an object just beyond Pluto and assumed it was another planet. He named it Eris. In addition to Eris, astronomers located a large number of small icy objects beyond Neptune that were similar to Pluto in both orbit and icy composition. This grouping of objects, known as the Kuiper belt, is believed by researchers to be the source of many comets.

The discovery of Eris led to astronomers to discuss and finally determine what makes a planet a planet. If Pluto was defined as a planet, then many of the objects in the Kuiper belt could also be called planets. A definition was finally determined. According to NASA, an object can be classified as a planet if it meet three specific criteria: first, it must orbit the sun; second, it must be big enough for gravity to squash it into a roundish ball; and third, it must have cleared other objects out of the way in its orbital neighborhood. Pluto failed to fulfill these requirements. On September 13, 2006, because of its distance from our sun and its size, Pluto was reclassified as a dwarf planet and grouped with the other objects found in the Kuiper belt.

cameras, which produce a thermal or heat-based image, astronomers can better identify possible exoplanets that exist in a Goldilocks zone.

There are three methods astronomers use to help detect exoplanets: the wobble method (also called the Doppler detection method), transit method, and the microlensing method.

The wobble method searches for changes in a star's speed, which is caused by the gravitational pull of a nearby planet. These changes in speed, both toward Earth and away from it, create variations in light that astronomers can detect. As a star pulses toward Earth, light waves are compressed, or are closer together. As its surges away from Earth, light waves widen and shift in color. This phenomena is called the Doppler effect. An eighteenth-century Austrian mathematician and physicist named Christian Doppler made this discovery. He first started using sound waves, but light also works the same way. Doppler found that waves traveling toward you would be compressed but were wider if they were moving away from you. If you listen to a train, the closer it gets, the sound of its whistle becomes a higher pitch. As a train gets closer to you, the sound waves are more compressed, creating the higher pitched sound. As the train travels away from you, its waves widen and its pitch lowers.

The transit method looks for light, and all planets block light. If one planet's orbit crosses between its sun and Earth, it blocks some of its sun's light and causes the star to dim in brightness. Telescopes that have sensitive photometers, which are high-powered instruments designed to detect variations in light, can easily identify large planets as well as smaller

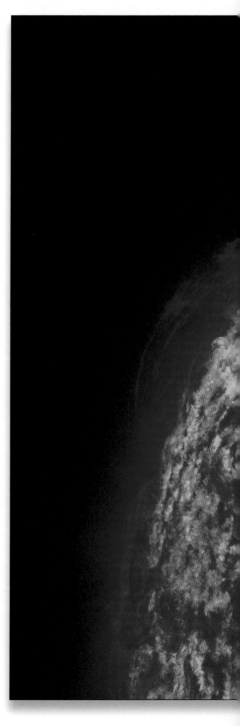

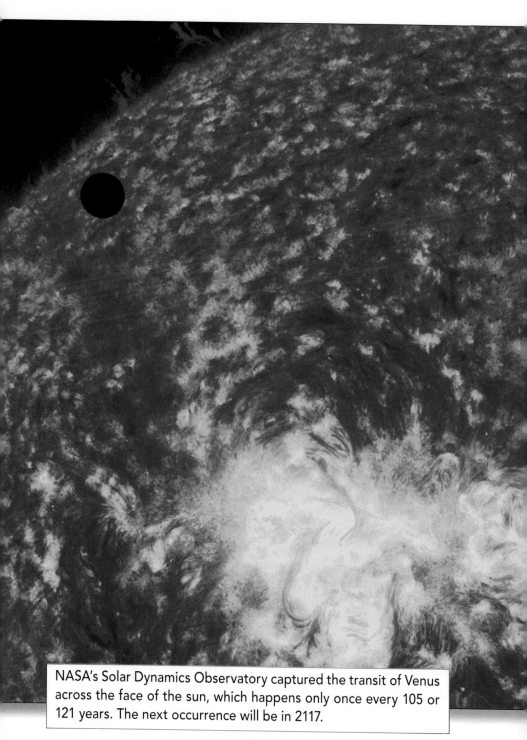

NASA's Solar Dynamics Observatory captured the transit of Venus across the face of the sun, which happens only once every 105 or 121 years. The next occurrence will be in 2117.

SCIENTISTS BELIEVE MOST STARS HAVE GOLDILOCKS ZONES

Based on research and data provided by the Kepler Telescope, scientists can now say with certainty that most stars have a Goldilocks zone. In the Milky Way alone, researchers have identified 1,800 exoplanets orbiting around stars in our galaxy. Some stars have more than one exoplanet orbiting them; as many as six planets have been identified as orbiting a star. All of these stars have habitable zones around them that are deemed by scientists to be far enough away to avoid being burning hot, yet close enough so that their entire surfaces are not covered in ice. Of course, a planet located within the Goldilocks zone does not mean is can support any form of life, human or otherwise, since atmospheric conditions must be evaluated. However, scientists are encouraged by the idea that within one of these inhabitable zones, the chance for life may exist.

ones by watching for any dimming in light by an object that is close to the size of Earth.

The microlensing method is used when a star passes directly in front of another star. When this happens, the gravity of the front star acts like a magnifying lens and intensifies the brightness of the star behind it. If a planet orbits the front star, the planet's additional gravity intensifies the effect and can reveal a planet.

WHO IS HUNTING PLANETS?

So who are the astronomers, astrophysicists, and researchers searching for planets in the Goldilocks zone? A number of major research organizations are leading the search for hospitable plants beyond the Milk Way. Together they hope to make significant discoveries as they share their results with scientists and other researchers around the world.

NASA

The National Aeronautics and Space Administration is an organization funded by the United States government. NASA oversees a space program and conducts aeronautics and aerospace research. NASA's Kepler program, which uses the Kepler Space Telescope,

Finding Planets With Microlensing

Astronomers use a technique called microlensing to find distant planets in the heart of our galaxy, up to tens of thousands of light-years away. This infographic illustrates how NASA's Spitzer Space Telescope, from its perch in space, helps nail down the distance to those planets.

A microlensing event occurs when a faint star passes in front of a distant, more visible star. The gravity of the foreground star acts like a magnifying glass to brighten the distant star. If a planet is present around the foreground star, its own gravity distorts the lens effect, causing a brief dip in the magnification.

The great distance between Earth and Spitzer helps astronomers determine the distance to the lensing planetary system. Spitzer can see lensing events before or after telescopes on Earth, and this timing offset reveals the distance to the system.

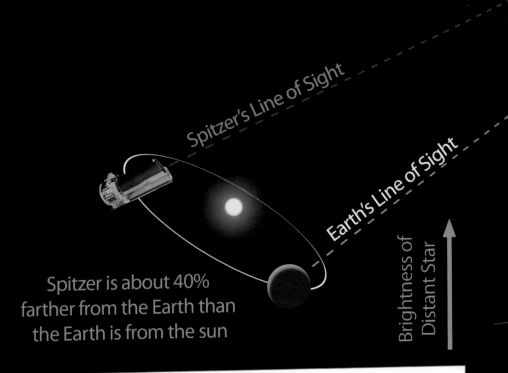

Spitzer's Line of Sight

Earth's Line of Sight

Spitzer is about 40% farther from the Earth than the Earth is from the sun

Brightness of Distant Star

This infographic illustrates how planets are discovered by NASA's Spitzer Space Telescope, which uses the microlensing technique.

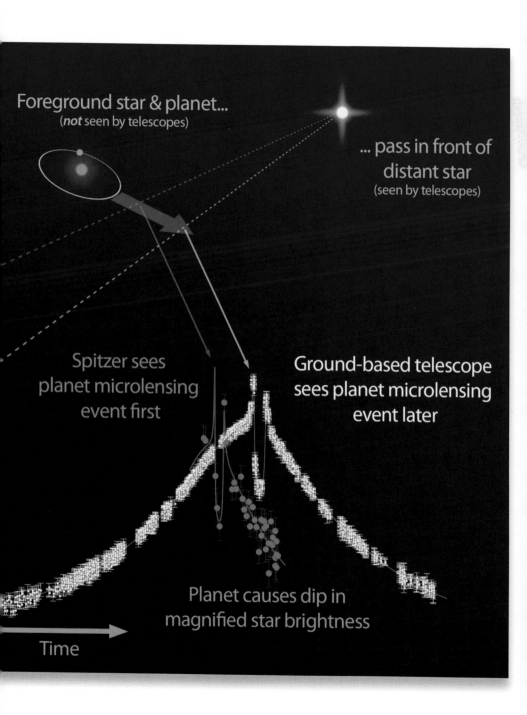

Foreground star & planet...
(*not* seen by telescopes)

... pass in front of
distant star
(seen by telescopes)

Spitzer sees
planet microlensing
event first

Ground-based telescope
sees planet microlensing
event later

Planet causes dip in
magnified star brightness

Time

is NASA's initiative to discover other Earth-like planets orbiting other stars in a Goldilocks zone. The Kepler Space Telescope, which was named for Renaissance astronomer Johannes Kepler, was launched on March 7, 2009, and is one of NASA's most celebrated programs. The Kepler Telescope continuously monitors more than 150,000 stars beyond our solar system and, as of January 2015, has discovered more than four thousand candidate planets using the transit method. A candidate planet is an object that, based on the transit method, meets all the criteria for being a planet. However, before one of these candidates can be confirmed as being an actual planet, it must be verified by scientific research. To date, eight candidate planets have been determined to be actual planets.

EUROPEAN ASTRONOMERS

In April 2007, European astronomers used the wobble method to discover, at that point, the most Earth-like planet ever found. The planet they found has been named Gliese 581c. It is roughly 12,000 miles (19,000 kilometers) in diameter, which is not much larger than Earth. However, its orbit around its sun is only thirteen days, which normally would suggest to scientists that its close proximity to its sun would make it a very, very hot planet. However, scientists have discovered that Gliese 581c's estimated surface temperature is similar to Earth's and ranges from 32 degrees Fahrenheit (0 degrees Celsius) to 102 degrees Fahrenheit (39 degrees Celsius). The research team also believes that the planet may have a developed atmosphere and could be entirely covered by water.

INTERNATIONAL ASTRONOMERS

In February 2012, an international team of scientists focused their research on a planetary object named GJ 667C, a dwarf star that has two other dwarf stars nearby. Originally, the research team was examining a previously dis-covered super-Earth, named GJ 667Cb, and came to discover GJ 667C, another super-Earth with an orbit of twenty-eight days.

The new planet, which sits within a known Goldilocks zone, receives 90 percent of the light that Earth receives. Based on its initial research, the team thinks GJ 667C may absorb the same amount of energy from its star that Earth absorbs from our sun and, therefore, may have liquid water on its surface. However, it may absorb more radiation, making it on the hotter end of the habitable zone than Earth.

An artist's rendition of Gliese 581g.

SPACE TELESCOPE SCIENCE INSTITUTE IN BALTIMORE, MARYLAND

In February 2012, this team published results from a massive project known as the PLANET (Probing Lensing Anomalies NETwork) Collaboration. Based on six years of microlensing observations, the institute's results may alter the way in which scientists search for planets. The study concluded that there are more Earth-like planets in the universe than gas giants, which was a wholly new concept to scientists. According to the study's authors, the Milky Way galaxy alone has the potential to contain more than 100 billion planets, 10 billion of which might be small, rocky, terrestrial planets like Mercury, Venus, Earth, and Mars. The study also revealed that more than 1,500 of these planets could be within fifty light-years of Earth. The impact of these findings is great and implies that in the Milky Way, one of billions of galaxies across the entire universe, the potential for other Earth-like planets to exist is great.

EUROPEAN SPACE AGENCY'S GAIA MISSION

On December 19, 2013, the European Space Agency launched a satellite named Gaia. The ESA is made up of twenty-two European countries (Austria, Belgium, Czech Republic, Denmark, Estonia, Finland, France, Germany, Greece, Hungary, Ireland, Italy, Luxembourg, the Netherlands, Norway, Poland, Portugal, Romania, Spain, Sweden, Switzerland, and the United Kingdom) that collaborate on research, discovery, and the development of Europe's space program. ESA's headquarters are in Paris, France, but the organization has sites in seven of its member countries.

Over a five year span, ESA is hoping Gaia will map out an accurate three-dimensional map of about one billion stars in the Milky Way, or roughly 1 percent of our galaxy's stars, in an attempt to learn more about the origin of the Milky Way and its evolution. Gaia will turn very slowly as it repeatedly scans the entire sky. Its goal is to examine one billion stars about seventy times each over the next five years. While Gaia is mapping out these stars, it will also measure key properties of each star, including its brightness, temperature, and chemical composition, which can tell us much needed information about our galaxy.

Gaia had its first major detection in August 2014, when it discovered its first stellar explosion, in a galaxy located 500 million light-years away.

CHAPTER FOUR

WHAT HAVE PLANET HUNTERS FOUND?

On January 6, 2015, NASA announced that the Kepler Space Telescope discovered its 1,000th planet. The Kepler mission has had a high volume of discoveries: Kepler has found more than half of all known exoplanets to date and has spotted 3,200 additional planet candidates, with scientists expecting to confirm about 90 percent of them as exoplanets that exist within their host star's Goldilock's zone.

MAJOR PLANETARY DISCOVERIES

Beginning in 1992 and 1995, when the first exoplanet was identified and confirmed, there have been major discoveries of planets within our solar system and within the greater universe that are located in a Goldilocks zone. Since its launch in 2009, the Kepler Space Telescope is behind the vast majority of these discoveries with more than 1,000 confirmed planets and another 500+ waiting to be verified.

2005

In 2005, researchers discovered a rocky, Earth-like planet that was 7.5 times larger than Earth and located about fifteen light-years away. Up until this point, the exoplanets that had been discovered were all larger than Uranus, the seventh planet in our solar system. The significance of this discovery is that it confirmed to astronomers that another rocky planet, besides Earth, orbits around a normal star in the universe.

2008

By 2008, the discovery of exoplanets had risen to 287 confirmed planets. The COROT Mission

HOW TELESCOPES WORK

The most important tool a scientist has when looking for planets is a telescope. A telescope is a scientific device used to magnify distant objects, such as stars, planets, and moons, in the sky.

Telescopes come in all different sizes, from small ones that can sit on a tri-pod in your backyard to enormous, multimillion-dollar telescopes housed at major research institutions and universities. They can be made from light plastic tubes or from several tons of metal and steel. There are two types of telescopes: the refractor telescope, which uses glass, and the reflector telescope, which uses mirrors.

In general, a telescope does two things: it collects light and magnifies an image. A telescope's ability to collect light depends on the diameter of its lens or mirror. The larger the lens or mirror, the more light it can collect. A telescope's magnification ability depends on how the lenses or mirrors are used together.

The largest telescope in the world, called the European Extremely Large Telescope (E-ELT), is being constructed and will debut in 2018. It will be located in Cerro Armazones, Chile.

The Hubble Space Telescope is an international project by two leading space agencies: NASA and the European Space Agency.

(Convection, Rotation and planetary Transits) announced the identification of two new exoplanets, both of which were gas giants. Most planetary finds until then were of gas giants, due to technology limits.

The Hubble Space Telescope would change this. In 2001, astronomers using this telescope made its first planetary detection when it came across the atmosphere of a planet orbiting a star outside our solar system.

TEN REMARKABLE EXOPLANETS

As researchers journey further in the universe, they are embarking on amazing discoveries of other planets. While researchers continue to search for habitable planets that may one day be colonized and called home, some fascinating planets have been found along the way. The ten most remarkable exoplanets include:

1. Epsilon Eridani b: Located only ten light-years from Earth, Epsilon Eridani b is a gas giant similar to Saturn or Jupiter. The planet is surrounded by two asteroid belts, which suggest to researchers that other Earth-like planets could exist on the inside of those belts, just as Earth exists in our own solar system.

2. Gliese 876d: This planet, while not at all inhabitable, does share a unique distinction as the first rocky super-Earth to be discovered and was the first evidence of other planets like our own existing elsewhere in the universe.

3. Gliese 581c: When it was discovered in 2007, Gliese 581c was the smallest exoplanet ever found. Due to its size, scientists thought it was likely rocky instead of gaseous. But researchers soon found that its orbit was outside of its star's Goldilocks zone and its surface too warm for liquid water.

4. GJ667Cc: An exoplanet confirmed in 2012, GJ667Cc is being called the best candidate for life in a habitable zone due to how perfectly the planet orbits its host star.

5. HD 40307 b: At forty-one light-years away, this is much closer to Earth than most exoplanets. Found using the wobble method, researchers have determined its size (more than four times the size of Earth), but they cannot yet figure out if it's rocky or gaseous.

6. GJ 1214b: The discovery of GJ 1214b is significant because astronomers think the planet may be one giant ocean, which means if liquid water is on its surface, the ability to support life may be possible as well. And, at only forty-one light-years from Earth, we can easily observe the planet to learn more.

7. Kepler-16b: What makes this planet unique is that it's a circumbinary planet, or a planet that orbits two different stars.

8. Kepler-10c: This planet is too hot to be habitable or to support life. However, the way it was discovered, using two different types of tools together, is what makes the planet unique. Using NASA's Spitzer Space Telescope along with software called Blender, scientists were able to discover and confirm this planet's existence. The new technique blends light from multiple sources around a potential planet and tracks the light over time to ensure the object researchers are looking at is in fact a planet and not another celestial body.

9. Kepler-11f: This planet is just one of many inside the Kepler-11 solar system. This solar system, found by the Kepler Telescope, is very compact. Five of its six planets orbit closer to that solar system's sun than any of the planets on our own solar system. Kepler-

(continued on the next page)

(continued from the previous page)

11f is more than two times the mass of Earth and is considered a super-Earth.

10. MOA-2007-BLG-192-Lb: As one of the smallest exoplanets ever discovered, MOA-2007-BLG-192-Lb, or MOA-192b for short, orbits a sun much smaller than our own and of a different makeup that does not make it a powerful heat source. MOA-192b is considered to be an icy, cold, gassy planet not suitable for life.

2009

Scientists announced the discovery of GJ 1214b, a planet like no other they have discovered before. It's big, 6.5 times more massive than Earth and 2.7 times wider. Scientists also believe the planet is made mostly of water and is covered by a thick, steamy atmosphere. GJ 1214b orbits a red dwarf star more than forty light-years from Earth.

2010

In March 2010, researchers announced another milestone: the discovery of a Jupiter-like planet located 1,500 light-years from Earth that was relatively cool and that could be studied in significant detail.

Because the COROT satellite discovered it, the planet was named COROT-9b. Other cool or colder planets had been found before COROT-9b, but this planet transits between its star and Earth. Using the transit method, scientists were able to study both its size (from the amount it diminished the light of its parent star) and the makeup of its atmosphere (from the way light interacted with the planet when light passed through its atmosphere). Scientists discovered that COROT-9b is located in its star's Goldilocks zone, but because the planet is mostly made up of gas, they do not believe it can support any forms of life.

In September 2010, a group of American astronomers using spectroscopic data, or information obtained by studying light and its wavelengths, from ground-based instruments announced that they had found a potentially hospitable planet. The discovery of the planet, named Gliese 581g because it orbits a star called Gliese 581, led to a lot of excitement because the planet was found so close to Earth. Two other planets had been previously found in the same red dwarf system (Gliese 581d and Gliese 581e), and both had orbits just outside of a habitable zone.

2011

January 2011 saw the

This illustration shows GJ 1214b, a super-Earth that orbits a star beyond our sun. Scientists can confirm that the planet has a thick atmosphere but cannot yet determine what it is made of.

Kepler mission confirm the discovery of its first rocky planet, estimated to be almost the same size as Earth and located inside a habitable zone.

In February 2011, Kepler scientists announced the discovery of five planets, each orbiting in the habitable zones of stars smaller and cooler than our sun. If confirmed, these five planets may represent the first planets of Earth-like size found in habitable zones. Also in February, Kepler located another six confirmed planets orbiting a sun-like star. To date, both discoveries make up the largest group of planets orbiting a single star ever discovered outside of our solar system.

The entire year was significant in the world of planet hunting as it produced more than seven hundred confirmed exoplanets.

2012

In March 2012, it was announced that a new dwarf planet, called 2012 VP113, was discovered just beyond Pluto, in the farthest reaches

WHAT HAVE PLANET HUNTERS FOUND?

of our solar system. It's full orbit is incredibly far away from the sun. Researchers are puzzled by 2012 VP113 and how it materialized since it's so far away from the sun yet still orbits the sun in a similar way to one of our solar system's planets.

2013

This proved to be a significant year for space discoveries. In addition to NASA's *Voyager I* reaching interstellar space after thirty-five years of travel, the discovery that Mars may have once supported life in the form of microbes, and the death of the "Comet of the Century" or Comet ISON, which broke apart after it passed by the sun, scientists also discovered a planet that's being called Earth's twin. Kepler-78b is slighter larger than Earth but has a similar density, which scientists believe means it's made out of similar rocky materials as Earth.

2015

On January 6, 2015, at a meeting of the American Astronomical Society, astronomers from the Harvard-Smithsonian Center for Astrophysics announced that they had identified eight new planets. Among the eight, the team has said, two are the most similar to Earth of any known exoplanets to date.

The two most Earth-like planets of the group are Kepler-438b and Kepler-442b. Both orbit red dwarf stars that are smaller and cooler than our sun. Kepler-438b is located 470 light-years from Earth, while the more distant Kepler-442b is 1,100 light-years away. Kepler-438b circles its star every 35 days, while Kepler-442b completes one orbit every 112 days.

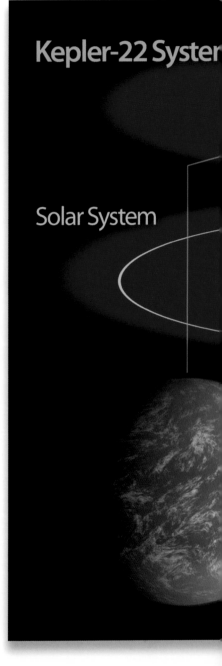

Kepler-22 System

Solar System

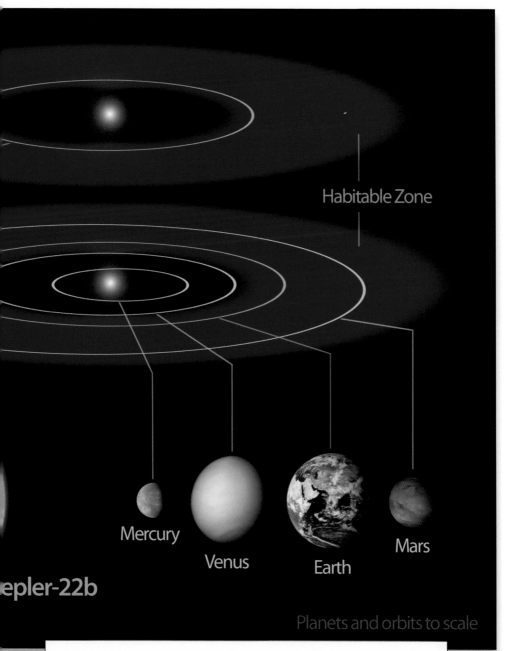

Habitable Zone

Mercury

Venus

Earth

Mars

epler-22b

Planets and orbits to scale

This diagram compares our solar system to the Kepler-22 system.

FUTURE MISSIONS

While the Kepler Space Telescope is continuing to identify more candidate planets, it's not the only telescope looking for other worlds. NASA plans to launch the Transiting Exoplanet Survey Satellite (TESS) in 2017. TESS will use the transit method to look for exoplanets and will focus its search on planets that are similar in size to Earth and only in Goldilocks zones. Once TESS makes a discovery, NASA will point the James Webb Space Telescope, which is set to launch in 2018, in the direction of Tess's discovery to learn more about each candidate planet's atmospheres. The James Webb will try to identify water vapor and gases, such as oxygen, nitrous oxide, and methane, to determine if the planet has any evidence of life.

NASA's plans for beyond 2018 include the construction and launch of the Wide-Field Infrared Survey Telescope. Two land-based telescopes—the HARPS spectrograph, on a telescope in Chile, and the HIRES spectrograph, on Hawaii's Keck Telescope—can both use the wobble method to detect possible exoplanets without the need to enter space.

The European Space Agency is currently reviewing three proposals that will survey, or study, the atmospheres of more than 500 exoplanets and the space around them. These possible missions—the Atmospheric Remote-Sensing Infrared Exoplanet Large-Survey (Ariel), the Turbulence Heating ObserveR (Thor), and the X-ray Imaging Polarimetry Explorer (Xipe)—would provide more information on the atmospheres of exoplanets, space phenomena such as space plasma physics, and X-ray emissions from high-energy supernovas and black holes.

CHAPTER FIVE

SEARCHING FOR LIFE

Since 1995, when the first exoplanet was discovered, the search for life on other planets has intensified and become a significant topic of interest. Over the past twenty years, the number of verified planets has continued to increase, creating new opportunities in the search for extraterrestrial life. Searching for life in the universe has also become an international initiative undertaken by a number of space organizations, including NASA.

NASA LAUNCHES MAJOR INITIATIVE

In April 2015, NASA announced the creation of NExSS, short for the Nexus for Exoplanet

System Science. As a result of the outstanding discovery of exoplanets by the Kepler mission, NExSS is an initiative that brings together scientists from three different NASA research centers (the NASA Ames Research Center, the NASA Exoplanet Science Institute, and NASA's Goddard Institute for Space Studies), the SETI (Search for Extraterrestrial Intelligence) Institute, and teams from ten different universities. The initiative is the agency's first formal attempt in several years to look for extraterrestrial intelligence. Making up the team will be earth scientists, who will study our home planet; planetary scientists, who will examine and research exoplanets within our solar system; heliophysicists, who will research, observe, and document how the sun interacts with orbiting planets; and astrophysicists, who will continue to develop data on existing exoplanets and the stars they orbit.

In the announcement from NASA, Jim Green, NASA's director of planetary science, said the NExSS project will provide "a synthesized approach in the search for planets with the greatest potential for signs of life. The hunt for exoplanets is not only a priority for astronomers, it's of keen interest to planetary and climate scientists as well."

HOW EXTREME LIFE ON EARTH EXTENDS TO THE HUNT FOR PLANETS

Under regular, or normal, circumstances here on Earth, there are three basic ingredients of life—water, organic compounds, such as hydrogen, oxygen or nitrogen, and energy. However, researchers have made significant discoveries, right here on Earth, of environments where there is a deficiency of these ingredients, and in some cases, no presence of them at all.

Finding extreme life here on Earth tells scientists what kind of conditions might suit life in other places in the universe. In the past thirty years, our knowledge of life in extreme environments has exploded. Scientists have found microbes that survive in nuclear reactors, microbes that thrive in acid, and even microbes that can swim in boiling-hot water. Whole ecosystems have been discovered around deep-sea vents that have never once seen sunlight and where water from these vents is so hot it can melt lead. These life-forms have unique physiologies. There are various systems that work to keep an organism alive. These systems have evolved in such a way that allow these organisms to survive and thrive in extreme environments. What all of this means is that each new example of an organism that sustains itself in an environment defined as extreme provides scientists with more evidence that life can exist in different environments in the universe that were previously not considered as life-sustaining.

MONO LAKE, CALIFORNIA

NASA scientists Richard Hoover and Elena Pikuta are among the many researchers who are on the hunt for extreme forms of life. They have discovered a new species of microorganism,

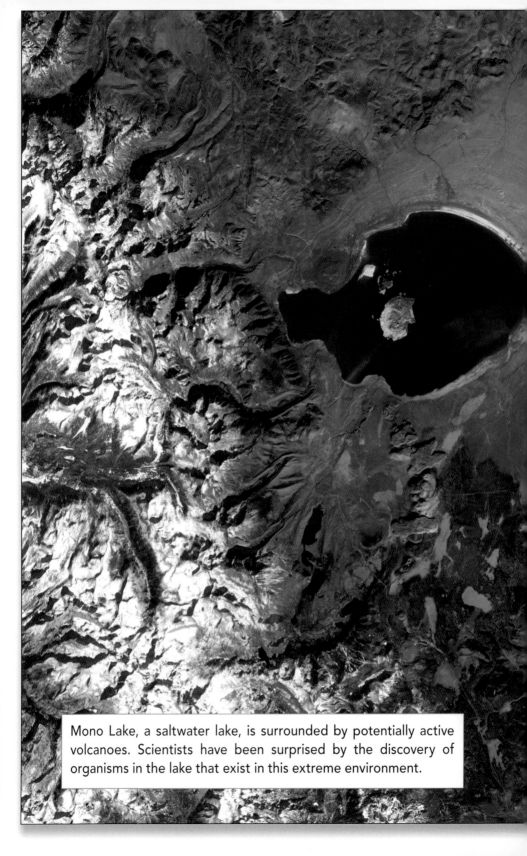

Mono Lake, a saltwater lake, is surrounded by potentially active volcanoes. Scientists have been surprised by the discovery of organisms in the lake that exist in this extreme environment.

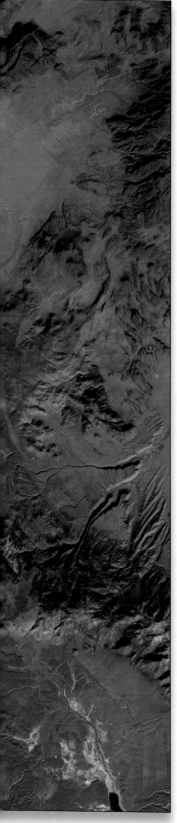

Tindallia californiensis, found in California's Mono Lake.

Mono Lake, which formed at least 760,000 years ago and is located near Lake Tahoe and Yosemite National Park, is an extremely salty and alkaline body of water. The lack of an outlet caused the lake to build up high concentrations of salt, making it almost three times saltier than seawater, with a pH of 10, which is about the same as the household cleaner Windex. However, within this body of water lives a recently discovered species of organism that thrives in the mud at the bottom of the lake. Mono Lake is home to millions of migratory and nesting birds, which feast on the small shrimp and other water life that live in and around the lake.

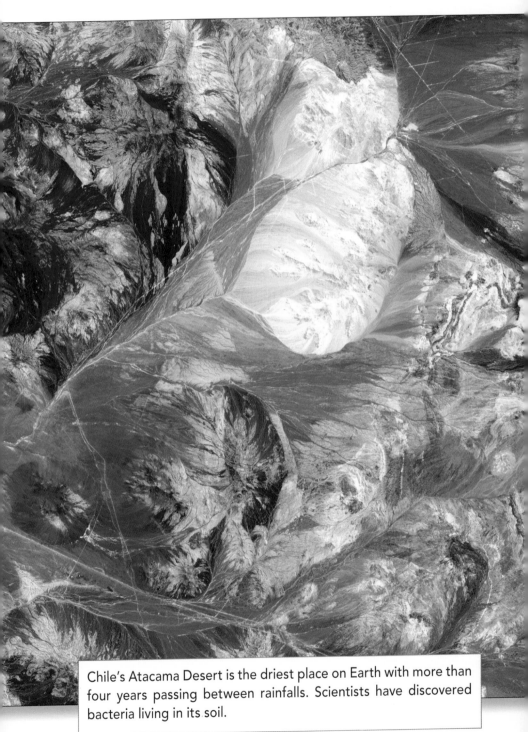

Chile's Atacama Desert is the driest place on Earth with more than four years passing between rainfalls. Scientists have discovered bacteria living in its soil.

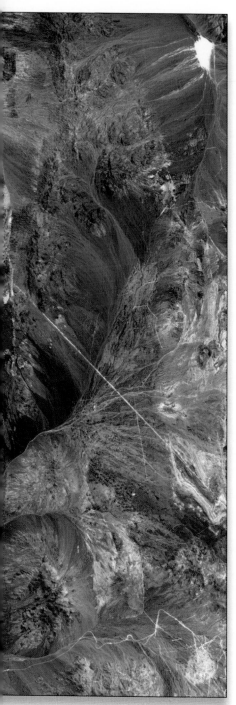

ATACAMA DESERT, CHILE

Located on the northern Andean plains of Chile sits the Atacama Desert, the driest place on Earth. In this desert, some researchers have found bacteria in the soil. The discovery is significant because the Atacama Desert's environment has many similarities to Mars. The discovery of this form of life in the desert means there is a strong possibility that bacteria or other microbes may exist in the soil on Mars, suggesting life can exist on the planet.

BEST BETS FOR LIFE IN OUR SOLAR SYSTEM

Our own solar system may end up being the place we find life beyond the confines of Earth. Four moons and one planet hold the potential to host some form of life.

Enceladus: The sixth-largest moon orbiting Saturn has been called one of the most promising objects in the solar system for life outside of Earth. The moon has a moderate temperature, and scientists say its surface of ice may have liquid water beneath it. NASA's Cassini Solstice mission in 2005 produced data that strongly suggests the moon has carbon, hydrogen, nitrogen, and oxygen within its atmosphere, all of which are elements essential for life to develop and survive.

Europa: This moon of Jupiter's has a frozen surface that may have water hiding beneath it, and its volcanic activity produces heat that many living organisms need to survive. Scientists are also studying evidence of microbial life that may exist in the moon's hydrothermal vents, which is similar to microorganisms found near these vents on Earth.

Mars: Known as the red planet, Mars's size and temperature range are both similar to Earth's. With large bodies of water located at its two poles, there is also strong evidence to suggest liquid water exists under the planet's surface. While the atmosphere is too thin to support human life, there is the potential for microbes to exist under its surface.

Titan: Saturn's largest moon exhibits evidence that it may have once had life living on its surface due to its thick atmosphere, which researchers have found to be rich in compounds that are often found with living organisms.

Io: Another moon of Jupiter's, Io is one of very few moons in our solar system that has an atmosphere, which happens to be made up of chemicals that support life. Among the best candidates to support life, Io does have a problem: it is constantly being hit by radiation, which makes its surface volatile and its temperature too cold.

GREAT SALT LAKE, UTAH

Great Salt Lake, located in the northern part of Utah, is divided into seven microenvironments, each with its own characteristics. The lake itself is the remnant of the ancient Lake Bonneville and is now divided in half, with most water flowing through the south arm of the lake, which produces a better living space for organisms commonly found near lake environments. The north arm, however, is a completely different environment. Because little water flows through the north arm, that portion of the lake traps more salt. Within this salty environment live halophilic, or salt-loving, microbes that produce red pigments called carotenoids. The carotenoids turn the lake water a pinkish-purple.

Within Yellowstone National Park, gurgling thermal pools of chemicals host life in the form of microscopic organisms.

YELLOWSTONE NATIONAL PARK, WYOMING

The bubbling acid hot springs of Yellowstone National Park are a vast habitat for thermophiles, or microorganisms that love the intensive temperatures of the volcanic activity that produces the water that thrusts up from the park's geysers. While the geysers are a popular tourist attraction for the park's visitors, they also happen to be habitats for microscopic organisms that live off the chemicals produced by the hot springs.

PACIFIC OCEAN (NEAR THE GALÁPAGOS ISLANDS)

Hydrothermal vents are cracks in Earth's crust where very hot water that has been heated beneath Earth's surface can escape. In the Pacific Ocean, near the Galápagos Islands, is vent water. Vent water may be superheated to over 750°F (400°C), it can be very acidic (similar to the strength of vinegar), and it contains a toxic mix

The Galápagos Islands host a giant tubeworm that lives in a hydrothermal vent that is too hot to support life and receives no light whatsoever from the sun.

of chemicals that includes heavy metals and sulphide. In this extreme environment is *Riftia pachyptila*, a giant tubeworm that can grow to more than seven feet long (two meters). This worm has no mouth or gut, but it does have a special organ that houses a type of bacteria that can convert carbon molecules into organic matter.

THE SEARCH FOR LIFE BEGINS AND ENDS ON EARTH

Earth's extreme environments host many organisms that thrive in a wide variety of very harsh conditions, such as dry deserts, toxic lakes, dark underwater caves, and acidic lakes and rivers. This proves to researchers that life can exist in extreme environments. These microbes—which scientists have named extremophiles—illustrate that life can adjust when it needs to survive. This discovery, and the examples that support it, have broadened scientists' understanding of the kinds of diverse environmental conditions in which life can survive, tolerate, and even thrive. As researchers examine exoplanets and their diverse environments, it is thought that the three basic ingredients scientists thought were needed to support life—water, organic compounds, and energy—may not apply to the search for extraterrestrial life, just as we have found that different kinds of life-forms exist right here on Earth. Similar extreme environments to those we have discovered here on Earth have also been discovered on different planets. This means that microorganisms and bacteria may survive there, too.

As scientists seek out Earth-like planets billions of light-years away, our search often brings us right back home, as we look more closely at Earth to find the answers to some of the universe's questions about the existence of extraterrestrial life. It has also caused many researchers to appreciate the variety of rare and unique conditions on Earth, which may, in the end, provide us with the clues we need to determine if life exists someplace else.

GLOSSARY

ASTRONOMER A scientist who studies stars, matter, and other objects in space.

ASTROPHYSICIST A scientist who studies the physical properties of the universe.

ATMOSPHERE An area of air and gas the surrounds objects in space, like stars, moons, and planets.

CIRCUMFERENCE The distance around something round.

DIAMETER The length of a straight line through the center of a circle.

EXTRASOLAR Originating outside our solar system.

FAHRENHEIT A temperature scale based on the freezing point of water (32 degrees) and the boiling point of water (212 degrees).

GEYSER A naturally occuring hot spring that

lets out a burst of water and steam when it boils.

KELVIN A unit of absolute temperature.

LIGHT-YEAR A unit for measuring the distance that light travels through space in one year.

MICROBE A tiny life-form.

MICROORGANISM An organism that is too small to be seen by the unaided eye.

ORBIT To move around an object in a circle.

ORIGIN The start, center, or beginning of something.

PHOTOSYNTHESIS The biological process in which plants use water and carbon dioxide to create food, grow, and release excess oxygen into the air.

PRINCIPLE A scientific theory that explains a

process or action.

RADIUS The measurement of a line from the center of a circle to its outside edge.

SOLAR SYSTEM A group of planets or celestial bodies that revolves around a sun.

TERRESTRIAL Relating to Earth or those who live there.

THERMOPHILE An organism that has adapted to living in an environment with extremely high temperatures.

FOR MORE INFORMATION

Canadian Space Agency
John H. Chapman Space Centre
6767 Route de l'Aéroport
Saint-Hubert, QC J3Y 8Y9
Canada
(450) 926-4800
Website: http://www.asc-csa.gc.ca/eng

The Canadian Space Agency coordinates all civil space-related policies and programs on behalf of the country of Canada.

European Space Agency
ESA HQ Mario-Nikis
8-10 rue Mario Nikis
75738 Paris Cedex 15
France
Website: http://www.esa.int

The European Space Agency (ESA) helps to shape the development of Europe's space capabilities and ensures investment in space, space exploration, and scientific discovery.

NASA
300 E. Street SW, Suite 5R30
Washington, DC 20546

(202) 358-0001
Website: http://www.nasa.gov
NASA is the United States' space agency and is focused on pioneering space exploration and scientific discovery.

NASA Ames Research Institute
Naval Air Station
Moffett Field
Mountain View, CA 94035
(650) 604-5000
Website: http://www.nasa.gov/centers/ames/
   home/index.html
The Ames Research Institute conducts world-class research and leads developments in aeronautics, exploration technology, and science.

NASA Goddard Space Flight Center
8800 Greenbelt Road
Greenbelt, MD 20771
(301) 286-2000
Website: http://www.nasa.gov/centers/
   goddard/home/index.html
The Goddard Space Flight Center is home to scientists, engineers, and technologists who build spacecraft and

design and develop instruments and new technologies to study Earth, the sun, our solar system, and the universe.

The Planetary Society
5 South Grand Avenue
Pasadena, CA 91105
(626) 793-5100
Website: http://www.planetary.org

The Planetary Society sponsors projects that will support innovative space technologies, nurtures creative young minds, and is a vital advocate for our future in space.

SETI (Search for Extraterrestrial Intelligence) Institute
189 Bernardo Avenue, Suite 100
Mountain View, CA 94043
(650) 961-6633
Website: http://www.seti.org

The SETI Institute explores and works to understand and explain the origin and nature of life in the universe.

SpaceX
SpaceX Headquarters

Rocket Road
Hawthorne, CA
(310) 363-6000
Website: http://www.spacex.com

SpaceX designs, manufactures, and launches advanced rockets and spacecraft in an effort to revolutionize space technology. The company's goal is to enable people to live on other planets someday.

WEBSITES

Because of the changing nature of Internet links, Rosen Publishing has developed an online list of websites related to the subject of this book. This site is updated regularly. Please use this link to access the list:

http://www.rosenlinks.com/SOE/Gold

FOR FURTHER READING

Aguilar, David A. *Space Encyclopedia: A Tour of Our Solar System and Beyond*. Washington, DC: National Geographic Children's Books, 2013.

Aguilar, David A. *13 Planets: The Latest View of Our Solar System*. Washington, DC: National Geographic Children's Books, 2011.

Anderson, Clyton C., and Nevada Barr. *The Ordinary Spaceman: From Boyhood Dreams to Astronaut*. Lincoln, NE: University of Nebraska Press, 2015.

Basher, Simon. *Astronomy: Out of This World!* New York, NY: Kingfisher/Pan Macmillian, 2009.

Basher, Simon. *Extreme Physics*. New York, NY: Kingfisher/Pan Macmillian, 2013.

Carney, Elizabeth. *National Geographic Kids: Planets*. Washington, DC: National Geographic Children's Books, 2012.

Discovery Kids. *The Universe.* New York, NY: Parragon Books, 2014.

DK Publishing. *Space: A Visual Encyclopedia.* New York, NY: DK Children, 2010.

Epstein, Brad, Alexandra Lee-Epstein, and Michael Lee-Epstein. *The Planets 101: The Solar System Unfolds.* Aliso Viejo, CA: Michaelson Entertainment, 2010.

Hawking, Stephen, Lucy Hawking, and Gary Parsons. *George and the Big Bang.* New York, NY: Simon & Schuster Books for Young Readers, 2013.

Hawking, Stephen, and Lucy Hawking. *George's Secret Key to the Universe.* New York, NY: Simon & Schuster Books for Young Readers, 2009.

James, Brian, and Russell Benfanti. *Eight Spinning Planets.* New York, NY: Cartwheel Books/ Scholastic Trade Division, 2010.

Ross, Jerry L., and Susan G. Gunderson. *Becoming a Spacewalker: My Journey to the Stars.* West Lafayette, IN: Purdue University Press, 2014.

Sagan, Carl. *Cosmos.* New York, NY: Ballantine Books, 2013.

Saucer, Carol. *A Space Science Journey: Explore the Cosmos Like Neil DeGrasse Tyson.* Amherst, NY: Prometheus Books, 2015.

Scott, Elaine. *Space, Stars and the Beginning of Time: What the Hubble Telescope Saw.* New York, NY: Clarion Books/Houghton Mifflin, 2011.

Sloan, Brian. *Flying! The Curious Kids Book About Airplanes, Aviation and Space Travel.* Seattle, WA: Amazon Digital Services, Inc., 2014.

Soluri, Michael, and John H. Glenn. *Infinite Worlds: The People and Places of Space*

Exploration. New York, NY: Simon & Schuster, 2014.

Tyson, Neil DeGrasse. *Death by Black Hole*. New York, NY: W. W. Norton & Company, 2014.

Tyson, Neil DeGrasse. *Origins: Fourteen Billions Years of Cosmic Evolution*. New York, NY: W. W. Norton & Company, 2014.

BIBLIOGRAPHY

Atkinson, Nancy. "Exoplanet Count Rises with New Discoveries." May 22, 2008. Retrieved June 23, 2015 (http://www.universetoday.com/14457/exoplanet-count-rises-with-new-discoveries/).

Drake, Nadia. "NASA's Kepler Spacecraft Discovers New Batch of Earthlike Planets." January 7, 2015. Retrieved June 21, 2015 (http://news.nationalgeographic.com/news/2015/01/150106-kepler-goldilocks-exoplanets-universe-space-science/).

European Space Agency. "Gaia Discovers Its First Supernova." September 12, 2014. Retrieved June 25, 2015 (http://sci.esa.int/gaia/54630-gaia-discovers-its-first-supernova).

European Space Agency. "Gaia: 'Go' for Science." July 29, 2014. Retrieved June 25, 2015 (http://sci.esa.int/gaia/54414-gaia-go-for-science/).

Freudenrich, Craig, PhD. "How Telescopes Work." Retrieved June 21, 2015 (http://science.howstuffworks.com/telescope7.htm).

Hsu, Jeremy. "10 Biggest Telescopes on Earth: How They Measure Up." December 29, 2011. Retrieved June 22, 2015 (http://www.space.com/14075-10-biggest-telescopes-earth-comparison.html).

Kim, Meeri. "Earth-size, 'Goldilocks-zone' Planet Found in Distant Solar System." April 17, 2014. Retrieved June 21, 2015 (http://www.washingtonpost.com/national/health-science/earth-size-goldilocks-zone-planet-found-in-distant-solar-system/2014/04/17/0bd7188c-c63b-11e3-8b9a-8e0977a24aeb_story.html).

Lamb, Robert. "How Do Planets Form?" Retrieved June 21, 2015 (http://science.howstuffworks.com/how-do-planets-form.htm).

Landau, Elizabeth. "Dwarf Planet Discovered at Solar System's Edge." March 27, 2014. Retrieved June 21, 2015 (http://www.cnn.com/2014/03/26/tech/innovation/dwarf-planet-solar-system/).

Lendino, Jamie. "Scientists: Most Stars Have 'Goldilocks' Planets in the Habitable Zone." March 20, 2015. Retrieved June 25, 2015 (http://www.extremetech.com/extreme/201671-scientists-most-stars-have-goldilocks-planets-in-the-habitable-zone).

Moskowitz, Clara. "Top 5 Bets for Extraterrestrial Life in the Solar System." January 14, 2009. Retrieved June 25, 2015 (http://www.wired.com/2009/01/et-life/).

NASA. "The Earth System." September 23, 2014. Retrieved June 21, 2015 (https://esw.climate.nasa.gov/2014/09/earth-system).

NASA. "NASA Rebooting Its Search for Life Beyond Earth Thanks to Exoplanets." April

28, 2015. Retrieved June 25, 2015 (http://www.aol.com/article/2015/04/26/nasa-rebooting-its-search-for-life-beyond-earth-thanks-to-exopla/21176618/).

NASA. "NASA's Kepler Marks 1,000th Exoplanet Discovery, Uncovers More Small Worlds in Habitable Zones." January 6, 2015. Retrieved June 21, 2015 (https://www.nasa.gov/press/2015/january/nasa-s-kepler-marks-1000th-exoplanet-discovery-uncovers-more-small-worlds-in).

NASA. "NASA's NExSS Coalition to Lead Search for Life on Distant Worlds." April 21, 2015. Retrieved June 2015 (http://www.nasa.gov/feature/nasa-s-nexss-coalition-to-lead-search-for-life-on-distant-worlds).

NASA. "What Is a Planet?" Retrieved June 25, 2015 (http://missionscience.nasa.gov/nasascience/what_is_a_planet.html).

National Geographic. "Lithosphere." Retrieved

June 21, 2015 (http://education.national-geographic.com/education/encyclopedia/lithosphere/?ar_a=1).

Sanders, Robert. "Astronomers Discover Most Earth-like Extrasolar Planet Yet." June 13, 2005. Retrieved June 23, 2015 (http://www.berkeley.edu/news/media/releases/2005/06/13_planet.shtml).

Sharp, Tim. "Mars' Atmosphere: Composition, Climate & Weather." August 3, 2012. Retrieved June 24, 2015 (http://www.space.com/16903-mars-atmosphere-climate-weather.html).

Tyson, Neil DeGrasse. "Goldilocks and the Three Planets." May 1, 1999. Retrieved June 21, 2015 (http://www.haydenplanetarium.org/tyson/read/1999/05/01/goldilocks-and-the-three-planets).

U.S. Environmental Protection Agency. "A Student's Guide to Global Climate Change:

The Greenhouse Effect." August 28, 2014. Retrieved June 21, 2015 (http://www. epa.gov/climatestudents/basics/today/ greenhouse-effect.html).

Wall, Mike. "Beyond Kepler: New Missions to Search for Alien Planets." May 2, 2013. Retrieved June 21, 2015 (http://www. space.com/20943-alien-planet-search-new-missions.html).

Williams, Matt. "10 Facts About the Milky Way." December 3, 2014. Retrieved June 21, 2015 (http://www.universetoday.com/22285/facts-about-the-milky-way/).

INDEX

helium, 12, 23
Herschel, William, 26
HIRES, 72
"hot Jupiter" planets, 23
hot springs, 33
Huang, Su-Shu, 28–30
Hubble Space
    Telescope, 61
hydrogen, 12, 23, 76
hydrosphere, 20

I

infrared cameras, 41, 43
infrared radiation, 19
intelligent life, search for,
    8, 26–27
Io, 83

J

James Webb Space Tele-
    scope, 72
Jupiter, 12, 14, 18, 23,
    36, 62

K

Kepler, Johannes, 50
Kepler-10c, 63
Kepler-11f, 63–64
Kepler-16b, 63
Kepler-78b, 69
Kepler-186f, 39

Kepler-438b, 70
Kepler-442b, 70
Kepler Space Telescope,
    25, 38, 39–41, 46, 47,
    50, 57, 58, 63, 66–68,
    75
Kuiper belt, 42

L

"Liquid Water Belt," 28
lithosphere, 19–20
Lowell, Percival, 27

M

Mars, 11, 14–16, 18,
    26–27, 36, 54, 69, 82
mass, what it is, 14
Mercury, 10, 14, 16, 18,
    36, 54
microbes, 6, 7, 20, 22, 33,
    69, 76–77, 88
microlensing method, 43,
    46–47, 54
microorganisms, 6, 85, 89
Milky Way, 12, 18, 30, 38,
    46, 47, 54, 55
MOA-2007-BLG-192-Lb,
    64
Mono Lake, 77–79
Morrison, Philip, 27

ABOUT THE AUTHOR

Laura La Bella is the author of more than twenty-five nonfiction children's books, including science titles such as Not Enough to Drink: Pollution, Drought, and Tainted Water Supplies and Safety and the Food Supply. La Bella, who was in the Young Astronauts Program in elementary school, has visited the Kennedy Space Center many times. She and her family live in Rochester, New York.

PHOTO CREDITS